BRITISH TRAMS

A PICTORIAL SURVEY

L. F. FOLKARD

D. BRADFORD BARTON LTD

Frontispiece One of Liverpool's smart streamlined double-deckers speeding along reserved track near Bowring Park in 1955. This route was destined to be Liverpool's last, and closed but two years later.

© Copyright D. Bradford Barton Ltd ISBN 085153 3280

Published by Enterprise Transport Books Ltd
3 Barnsway, Kings Langley, Hertfordshire WD4 9PW

Printed and bound in Great Britain by BPC Hazell Books Ltd

CONTENTS

INTRODUCTION

At the end of the Second World War, some thirty towns and cities in the United Kingdom possessed electric tramway systems, and in addition there were a few 'interurban' tramways which preferred to call themselves electric railways, such as the Grimsby & Immingham, the Llandudno & Colwyn Bay, and the Manx Electric. There were also such gems as the Douglas horse tramway and the Great Orme cable tramway, both happily still with us, while over in the Irish Republic, trams could be found in Dublin and on the nearby Hill of Howth.

Unfortunately several of the surviving tramways were remnants of larger systems which had been lingering on because of the war, with worn-out equipment, and these closed as soon as replacement vehicles became available.

There were no general abandonment plans in respect of the major tram systems at Liverpool, Leeds, Sheffield, Blackpool, Sunderland, Glasgow, Edinburgh, Aberdeen and Dundee, and the future of trams in these places for a time seemed reasonably secure. However, this was not to be, and one by one the last strongholds fell. New trams were very expensive and few firms were interested in tendering for them; mass-produced diesel buses seemed a cheaper and more attractive proposition to the local authorities who ran the tramways, and the whole question soon became political.

Trolleybuses as an alternative had ceased to become attractive, the argument often being propounded that buses were 'more flexible' than trams or trolleybuses. Little attempt to apply modern tramway principles was made; even by the early 1950s many of Europe's war-torn cities had tramways to be proud of, with much segregated track and new, high-capacity single-deck cars, but our City Fathers did not wish to know about them.

With the closure of Glasgow's last route in 1962, electric trams remained only at Blackpool and on the Manx Electric Railway. A 2ft. gauge pleasure line was in operation at Eastbourne, and there were the Douglas horse trams and the Great Orme cable trams. Up and down the country, small but dedicated groups of enthusiasts were pre-serving and restoring what they could salvage of the tramway era.

Today the situation is perhaps a shade happier; Blackpool and the Isle of Man still have trams, and the Eastbourne enterprise has moved bodily to Seaton and expanded. A magnificent collection of restored trams is on show at the Crich Tramway Museum in Derbyshire, which has the great attraction of being a working museum where one can actually ride the trams. On the debit side, the Museum of British Transport at Clapham, which contained several trams, has been closed and the exhibits dispersed.

Smaller preservation schemes featuring working tramways are to be found at Carlton Colville, near Lowestoft, and at Beamish in County Durham, while various private restoration projects for individual cars are in progress. With a few honourable exceptions, it has been the enthusiasts and not the former tram-operating authorities who have ensured that examples of the typical British tramcar have been preserved for posterity.

Perhaps the most significant recent development has been the construction of the Tyne & Wear Metro, which though in no way resembling earlier British tramway practise, has been hailed as 'Supertram', and will be very akin to the light rapid-transit systems which have evolved from some of the Continental tramways, particularly those in West Germany.

The illustrations in this volume have been selected with the object of showing as many types as possible of the trams which operated in Britain and Eire within the last quarter of a century, and a selection from all systems still running in 1952 has been included.

Grateful thanks are due to those who have contributed photographs and information, particularly to W. J. Wyse Esq., B.Sc, who is Chairman of the Light Railway Transport League, as well as to fellow-members of that excellent Society.

Leslie F. Folkard
Torquay

LONDON Ownership of all trams within the London area was vested in the London Passenger Transport Board in 1933, and they soon embarked on a policy of replacement by trolleybuses and buses, until the last trams ran in 1952. No.204, seen on the Victoria Embankment - the longest of London's few stretches of reserved track – was an E3 class car, built in 1931 for Leyton Council to the same design as cars supplied in the previous year to London County Council. The slot between the rails gave access to the underground conduit from which the cars took their current by means of a collector shoe or 'plough'. Many cars were also fitted with trolley poles, as most routes changed to overhead collection at the outer ends.

Among the municipal constituents of London Transport were the East Ham, West Ham, Croydon and Walthamstow Council Tramways, who ran bogie cars very similar to the London County Council E1 class, but with a superior internal finish. No.94 was an East Ham car, transferred south of the river after the routes through the East End closed, and is seen in Greenwich heading for its new home at Abbey Wood depot, whose allocation latterly consisted almost entirely of ex-East Ham and West Ham cars.

[W. J. Wyse]

The most numerous type of tram in London was the E1 class maximum-traction bogie car, of which 1050 were built between 1907 and 1930 for the London County Council. Drivers' screens were not fitted until the late 1930s, although a lot of E1s were scrapped during that decade and never received them. After the war, many cars were in a deplorable state, and some had to be fitted with temporary bracing which is visible on the side of No.1802 when photographed on the traverser at Penhall Road, where cars withdrawn in the South London conversion programme were scrapped. [W. J. Wyse]

One of the most notable features of the London tramways was the Kingsway Subway, which opened in 1906/8 and ran from the Embankment to Bloomsbury, with underground tram stations at Holborn and Aldwych. Originally built for single-deckers, it was deepened in 1930/1 for double-deck operation, and thereafter cars of the E3 type worked most of the services through it, though the HR2 type car such as No. 1862 in this illustration also appeared regularly. The two types had identical bodies, but whereas the E3s had maximum-traction bogies and two motors, the HR2s were more powerful cars with equal-wheel bogies and four motors, as they were intended for working hilly routes. Three HR2s were sold to Leeds in 1939, and the trucks and equipment of many more went to Egypt after the war. One HR2 is preserved at Carlton Colville.   [W. J. Wyse]

London Transport rehabilitated over 100 of the old L.C.C. E1 class cars in the 1930s, giving them flush side panels, inset destination boxes, and drivers' screens. These rebuilds were reclassified E1R, and one of them is seen at New Cross Station, not far from London's last operational tram depot.
[W. J. Wyse]

CITY & SOUTHWARK
VIA BRIXTON

2079

Two of London Transport's constituent companies, the London United and the Metropolitan Electric Tramways shared a hundred maximum-traction bogie trams built in 1930/1 by the Union Construction & Finance Co Ltd of Feltham. These cars, referred to as the Felthams, were a considerable improvement on any others running in London, having fully-enclosed drivers cabs at a time when most drivers were still exposed to the elements. When new, the L.U.T. cars worked on the long route to Uxbridge, and the M.E.T. batch on the routes northward to Barnet and Enfield, but all migrated south of the river when these routes closed, and ran on the Streatham/Tooting and Purley routes. Most of the Felthams gained a new lease of life when they were sold to Leeds in 1951. This picture shows No.2079 on the awkward terminus situated at the end of Southwark Bridge, which appeared on the destination blinds as 'City & Southwark'.

[W. J. Wyse]

London Transport No.1 was an experimental car built in 1932 at the L.C.C.'s Charlton works on E.M.B. heavyweight bogies purloined from an HR2-class car. It was known as the Bluebird on account of the blue livery which it bore until 1937, when it was repainted in the standard red and cream. No. 1 made history in 1938 when it ran from Waltham Cross to Purley and back, a round trip of nearly sixty miles on a special organised by the Light Railway Transport League. It was sold to Leeds in 1951 for further service alongside ex-London 'Feltham' and HR2 cars, and is now preserved.   [W. J. Wyse]   13

BIRMINGHAM   Birmingham tramways were of 3ft. 6in. gauge, and their showpiece was the Bristol Road, along which the trams ran for miles uphill and down dale on reserved track. The last four-wheelers were withdrawn in 1949, and until the final closure in 1953 the remaining routes were worked by maximum-traction bogie cars, all of the same general design, built between 1913 and 1929. Their livery was dark blue and cream with maroon trucks, and most cars had red glass toplight windows. No.736 when photographed was bound for Rednal with a good load of passengers.   [W. J. Wyse]

14

The narrow profile of the Birmingham trams is clearly shown in this view of No.791 leaving Martineau Street for Alum Rock, as is the bow collector which was replaced in 1950 by a trolley pole when the route closed and its cars were transferred to the Bristol Road. The centre of Birmingham has now been redeveloped, and nothing remains of the street or the buildings in the picture.

[P. W. Gray]

SHEFFIELD Sheffield's tramways were noteworthy for their many steep hills and for their fleet of smart four-wheeled double-deckers. No.75 was one of over two hundred standard cars built between 1928 and 1936, mostly by Sheffield C.T. on Peckham P22 trucks. It was photographed at Fitzalan Square in the city centre on a wintry day in 1959, by which date several tram routes had already been closed.

An earlier generation of Sheffield trams was represented by the 150 cars built by Brush and Craven, also on Peckham P22 trucks, between 1919 and 1927. These all retained the old blue and cream livery – which could still be seen until 1958 – as exemplified by No.385, although a lot of the newer cars received the cream and blue livery which was applied from 1936 onwards.

The newest cars in the Sheffield fleet were the 'Jubilee' cars built in 1950-2 by Roberts on Maley & Taunton trucks, but they suffered a premature demise when the last routes closed in 1960. Two have been preserved, of which one is No.510, photographed at Handsworth in 1952 when quite new. This car is now at Crich Tramway Museum in company with two other typical Sheffield double-deckers.

Several Sheffield trams were destroyed in air raids, and to replace them the Corporation built new domed-roof cars to practically the same design as a batch constructed between 1936 and 1939. Wartime car No.85, just out of the paint shop, is seen at Intake terminus in 1952.

To ease a wartime stock shortage, Sheffield purchased fourteen 1901-vintage cars from Newcastle in 1941 and rebuilt them as all-enclosed. The 'Tudor Arch' saloon windows were a feature of many trams built in the early years of the century.

[W. J. Wyse]

GRIMSBY AND IMMINGHAM A seven-mile long electric light railway was opened in 1912 by the Great Central Railway, and provided a direct service between Grimsby and Immingham Docks, with a short branch to Immingham Town. The tracks ran in the street at either end, but most of the run was on track laid to railway standards. The line came under the wing of the LNER at the grouping, and on nationalisation passed to British Railways, who closed it in 1961 despite heavy peak-hour traffic.

The upper photograph shows a group of cars at Corporation Bridge terminus, Grimsby, including No.1, built by Brush in 1911 and still in faded LNER teak livery. Most cars eventually received BR malachite green livery with lion-and-wheel emblem. No.6 in the lower photograph was one of three cars purchased from Newcastle Corporation in 1948. It was built in 1901 by Hurst Nelson and rebuilt in 1932/3.

[J. H. Meredith]

19

LIVERPOOL The standard four-wheeled 'Priestley' cars were built by the Corporation in large numbers during the 1920s. No.754, seen on a morning peak hour working at Old Haymarket, was one of the last in service, and was not withdrawn until 1952. It was slightly longer than most of its type, and in addition had received various modifications such as the distinctive E.M.B. hornless truck and the very large route number indicator. Most of the 'standards' were built without drivers screens and some never received them.

No.764 was one of twelve bogie cars built in 1931, of which most were rebuilt with E.M.B. lightweight bogies and the large standard indicator display. As with the 'standard' four-wheeled cars, livery was originally maroon and cream, but became green and cream in the mid 1930s and finally green and light grey. Some lasted until 1955. The reserved track at Bowring Park was typical of the Liverpool suburbs, and speeds unheard of on many systems were regularly attained.

Twelve bogie cars built in 1933 on E.M.B. heavyweight bogies were the first to appear in the green livery. Body styling was noticeably more modern than on their immediate predecessors, though details varied within the batch, for instance No.778 was one of four to have a domed roof.

[W. J. Wyse]

No. 792 was one of the Robinson 'Cabin' bogie cars built in 1934, with the unaccustomed luxury of a fully-enclosed drivers compartment, and, for the period, the unusual feature of reversed staircases which faced the back of the car. Most had E.M.B. heavyweight bogies of the Johannesburg type, and the majority of this series of cars were reconditioned after the war and lasted until 1953-5.

The 'Marks bogie' cars of 1935/6 were very similar in appearance to their predecessors the Robinson 'Cabin' cars, but had normal stairs and cabs. They deteriorated into a very poor state due in no small measure to the war and to the rough track on the routes through Bootle which they normally worked, but most were reconditioned after these routes closed in 1949 and they gave a few more years service. No.852, with E.M.B. lightweight bogies, is depicted at Old Haymarket.

Liverpool trams were collectively known as 'Green Goddesses', and in 1936/7 a series of 163 streamlined bogie cars were produced which were truly worthy of the name. They were also sometimes known as 'Liners', and No.155, photographed in full sail down William Brown Street, was one of those fitted with E.M.B. lightweight bogies, while others had E.M.B. heavyweight or Maley & Taunton bogies. A disastrous fire at Green Lane depot in 1947 destroyed 22 of these cars, and a further 46 were sold to Glasgow in 1953/4 for further service. The last ones in Liverpool were withdrawn late in 1956 when the long routes to Kirkby closed, leaving the four-wheeled streamline cars to work out the last few months on the remaining routes. One of the cars which went to Glasgow, No.869, has returned to Liverpool for preservation and is being restored by the Merseyside Tramcar Preservation Society. The streamliners were extremely comfortable cars, and the lower view shows the brown leather swing-over seating on the top deck of No.872.

The hub of Liverpool's tram system was at Pierhead, on the site of the former George's Dock, where the Liver and Cunard buildings dominated the skyline and many of the city's tram routes terminated on three turning circles adjoining the landing stages of the various Mersey ferries. This illustration shows Nos.287 and 273, two of the 100 four-wheeled streamlined cars, sometimes known as 'Baby Grands' which were built between 1937 and 1942. Ten of this type, including the short-lived No.300, perished in the Green Lane depot fire of 1947, but most of the remainder survived until the closure of the Liverpool tramways, and it was cars of this type which made the final procession on that sad day, 14 September 1957. The official last car, No.293, went to the U.S.A. for preservation, and No.245 is preserved in Liverpool.

LEEDS had an extensive tram system which originated from Britain's first overhead-wire electric route opened in 1891. Many of the routes had long stretches of reserved track, such as that at Oakwood on the Roundhay route on which No.42 is depicted. This car was one of two hundred 'Chamberlains' built in 1927 by Brush, English Electric and Leeds C.T. on E.M.B. pivotal trucks. These trucks were in effect two one-axle bogies and after a few years were secured or the cars retrucked due to their alarming tendency to pivot the wrong way!

[W. J. Wyse]

Over a hundred 'Horsfield' cars like No.194, seen leaving Gipton Estate, were built in 1930/1 by Leeds Corporation and Brush, mostly on Peckham P35 trucks. Though unspectacular, they were solid and reliable, many lasting until tramway operation in Leeds ceased in November 1959. Leeds trams, like L N E R locomotives, had class numbers and subdivisions, the 'Horsfield' variants being classes C1, C2, C1/2, etc. No.180 of this type is preserved at Crich Tramway Museum.

A large housing estate was built at Middleton, on the outskirts of Leeds, in the 1930s and to serve it a new tramway on private track was constructed, running for much of its route through woodland. To work the route, the 'Middleton bogie' cars were built by Brush and English Electric on Maley & Taunton heavyweight bogies. No.262, by then in red livery which had replaced the earlier blue, was photographed in the woods on a bleak November day in 1955. These excellent cars were scrapped in 1956/7 and regrettably none were preserved.

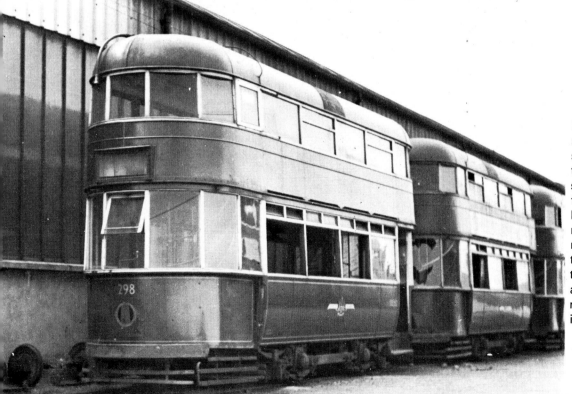

Leeds purchased secondhand cars from several operators, among the more distinctive and shortest-lived being these from Southampton. The low height and domed roof were required to enable the cars to run through the Bargate in their home town. No.298 and two sisters are seen here awaiting scrap after little more than two years service in Leeds.

Two non-standard cars seen together in City Square are No.276, the solitary example of class J1/WT 28s, which was built by Leeds C.T. in 1948 utilising spare parts, and No.274 of class E1/2, one of three four-wheeled streamlined cars built in 1935 by Leeds C.T. on Maley & Taunton trucks. The frontal styling earned this trio the nickname of 'Lance Corporals'.   [W. J. Wyse]

Two magnificent 'railcoaches' were built in 1953, with single deck, centre-entrance bodies by Roe seating but 34 passengers. One had EMB lightweight bogies, and No.602 as illustrated had inside-bearing bogies by Maley & Taunton. They were painted in a distinctive purple livery, but their use was rather limited due in no small measure to their incompatibility with the rest of the fleet. They did however work the short route to Hunslet for a time in company with a third single-decker which had been heavily rebuilt from an ex-Sunderland car. Crich Tramway Museum is now the home of No.602.

Leeds purchased 90 of the 'Feltham' type maximum-traction bogie cars from London Transport in 1950/1, though not all saw further service. They had been built in 1930/1 for the Metropolitan Electric and London United Tramways, and were of unusual design with fully-enclosed drivers cabs which projected beyond the body proper. They were fast and comfortable vehicles and could really show their paces on the Leeds tracks with their long stretches of unobstructed reservations. No.525 is seen in Middleton woods early in 1959, a few months before closure. One of these cars is preserved in London.

Most systems had a variety of works cars, whose duties included shunting, railgrinding, stores or staff transport, overhead inspection, permanent way duties, snow clearance, and mess accommodation, to name but a few! No.2 was a stores car attached to the Leeds Permanent Way Department, in whose Sovereign Street yard it was photographed.

[W. J. Wyse]

SUNDERLAND was noteworthy for the great variety of trams to be found in its fleet; out of 95 cars latterly in service, there were at least 23 visibly different types! The older cars were all rebuilt and re-equipped during the 1930s, and one curious rebuild was No.61, originally an open-topped car built in 1920, which was given a very short top saloon in 1934, and was known as the 'Ice Box' or the 'Turret Car'.
[W. J. Wyse]

Among the most modern cars in the fleet were a few four-wheeled, centre-entrance streamlined double-deckers built at the Corporation's Hylton Road works in 1936-40, and No.53 of this series was photographed beside the sea at Seaburn terminus in 1951. Livery was red and cream, and most cars featured the inverted 'V' front styling, whilst the entire fleet exhorted one to shop at Binns! [W. J. Wyse]

The nearest Sunderland came to having a standard type was the construction of twelve cars in 1934 known as the 'Wearsiders', and even this order was shared between two builders! Mounted on E.M.B. trucks, these cars were somewhat unsymmetrical in having toplights to the upper deck windows but not the lower. They outlived several newer cars, and most survived until closure of Sunderland's last route in 1954. [W. J. Wyse]

Twelve cars built in 1921/2 were the first in Sunderland to be totally enclosed, and in their original condition had front exits, though they lost these when rebuilt and retrucked in the early 1930s. No.82 is seen approaching the Wheatsheaf junction from the Roker direction.

[W. J. Wyse]

The modernisation programme of the 1930s was assisted by the purchase of fairly new cars from other undertakings. No.30 was one of eight built for Huddersfield Corporation by English Electric in 1931, and sold to Sunderland in 1938. They proved to be a good buy, and went into service without even a repaint. All but one lasted until the closure of the system. [W. J. Wyse]

No.26 was one of three rather handsome four-wheelers having domed-roof bodies with rooflights, and was built by Sunderland Corporation in 1935. This trio were among the first cars in the fleet to carry the pantograph collectors, so common on the continent but rare in Britain. This is a view taken on the Durham Road reserved track, which was a post-war extension to the system. [W. J. Wyse]

No.6 was one of a batch of eight four-wheelers obtained secondhand from London Transport in 1938. They had been built by Brush for Ilford Council and although only dating from 1932 did not have enclosed driving platforms until they came to Sunderland, whose workshops also fitted pantographs, reduced the height of the lower saloons, and later retrucked them. With these modifications, they ran until 1954.

[W. J. Wyse]

No.48 was a solitary centre-entrance car built by Brush in 1936 on a Maley & Taunton truck and purchased by Sunderland from South Shields in 1946. It is seen at the Wheatsheaf junction, passing the tramway offices, the larger of the Corporation's two depots lying just out of sight to the right. Among other secondhand purchases were a batch of 'Pilcher' cars from Manchester – this type is illustrated on page 51 – and a few odd cars from Accrington, Bury, and Portsmouth.   [W. J. Wyse]

The great variety within the Sunderland fleet is very evident from this depot view. A noteworthy car on the left is No.100, a bogie centre-entrance car, which was also ex-London Transport and was one of the prototypes from which the 'Feltham' type cars were developed. It has been preserved at Crich Tramway Museum, though unfortunately all the more typical Sunderland cars were scrapped.   [W. J. Wyse]

GLASGOW possessed the second largest tram system in the British Isles, and did not close its last route until 1962. For many years, the fleet consisted largely of 'standard' four-wheel double-deckers built between 1898 and 1924, which once numbered 1000. There were latterly three main distinguishable variants, No.358 being one having round dash panels and toplights to the lower deck windows. It was photographed in 1954 at Elderslie, near the end of one of the very long routes which it was possible to ride for 4d.

Another variation of the 'standard' car was the hexagonal dash type, built between 1910 and 192_ originally having open vestibule ends to the top deck. No.68, with one of the lady drivers employed i_ large numbers in the 1950s, is seen in Argyle Street having just passed beneath Central Station.

[P. W. Gray

Yet another variant of Glasgow 'standard' had a round dash, but the lower saloon had a monitor roof with a perforated metal ventilator strip instead of the glass half-lights. No.812, restored to pre-war livery, stands at Crich Town End, terminus of the Tramway Museum Society's line in Derbyshire.

[C. H. S. Owen]

Until the second world war, Glasgow trams had their top decks painted different colours according to the route on which they worked; these 'Kilmarnock Bogies' built in 1927/8 were 'red' cars used on East-West routes with few curves. No.1138 is seen at Dalmuir West in 1952.

Glasgow had a larger fleet of works trams than some towns had of passenger cars! A local speciality was a batch of Permanent Way Dept sand and sett cars, such as No.37, purpose built in 1935. The works car fleet used to congregate at Langside depot where about fifteen of them were based and where this photograph was taken.

[W. J. Wyse]

One of the 'Kilmarnock Bogies', No.1100, was rebuilt in 1941 with streamlined ends, but the result was not particularly pleasing aesthetically, in fact the car was known to some as the 'Horrornation'! It is depicted receiving depot attention while 'Standard' No.812 passes by. The scene, however, is not in Glasgow, but at the Crich Tramway Museum.

Glasgow built 152 of these 'Coronation' cars in their Coplawhill workshops between 1937 and 1941, plus another six in 1954. Livery was orange, cream and green, with less maroon relief than on the older cars, and most had E.M.B. lightweight bogies. They survived until 1961/2, and examples have been preserved of these and most other Glasgow types, both in the Scottish Transport Museum, situated in the works where most of the cars were built, and at the Crich Tramway Museum. The photograph shows Nos.1236 and 1202 in Renfield Street at the junction with Sauchiehall Street in 1958.

Glasgow purchased 46 of the Liverpool 'Goddesses' in 1953/4 and after slight modifications such as removal of fenders they were put into service on route 29 (Broomhouse - Milngavie) to which they were virtually restricted because of clearance difficulties. Car No. 1008, seen at Broomhouse in 1954, was one of the batch with Maley & Taunton bogies. The 'Goddesses' had a short life in Glasgow, being withdrawn in 1958-60, though one has returned to Liverpool for preservation.

The principal post-war additions to the Glasgow fleet were the 100 'Cunarders', built in 1948-52 at Coplawhill works on Maley & Taunton inside-bearing bogies. The majority of these fine cars ran until the closure of the last route in 1962, though some had been lost in a depot fire during the previous year. No. 1377 was photographed late one summer evening in 1958 nearing the Bellahouston terminus of route 7, one of the few which did not penetrate the city centre. A section of this route was sometimes referred to as 'The Glory Road', as it served the districts where some of the city's toughest citizens resided!

EDINBURGH No large-scale electrification of Edinburgh's tramways took place until 1922/3 when the city's extensive cable car system closed. Some cable cars were converted to electric traction, but new 'standard' cars such as No.64 were built in large numbers, being produced by various manufacturers. Livery was maroon and cream, with varnished window surrounds and gold lining.

Edinburgh's best-known thoroughfare is Princes Street, and most of the tram routes traversed it. 'Streamline' car No.12, which was photographed on route 12 in Princes Street near Waverley Station, was one of twenty all-steel cars supplied in 1935 by three different builders. Their trucks were latterly all the standard Edinburgh P22 Peckham type, but several at various times had the Maley & Taunton swing link truck. All ran until 1956.

[W. J. Wyse]

These handsome cars were built in Edinburgh's Shrubhill Works between 1934 and 1950 on Peckham trucks. No.189 was photographed on a wet day at Fairmilehead terminus, well up into the hills south of the city, shortly before the closure of the last routes in 1956. The two lights under the route number showed a route colour code.

Although the Edinburgh fleet in post-war years was highly standardised, a few odd cars could always be seen. Among them was No.260, a distinctive though hardly handsome design built by Metro-Cammell in 1933.

[W. J. Wyse]

Four streamlined cars were built for Aberdeen in 1940 by English Electric, of which two were centre-entrance bogie cars and two were four-wheelers on E.M.B. trucks. More of the bogie type were built after the war, but the single-truck cars remained odd men out in the fleet. No. 140 was photographed at Woodside terminus, beyond which point a separate company's trams once operated.

Double-deckers with open balcony ends to their top decks were once common in Britain, and late survivors were the Aberdeen cars which ran until the early 1950s. No. 92 was one of a batch built in 1920/1 by Aberdeen C.T. on Brill 21E trucks.
[C. Carter]

The standard
Aberdeen all-enclosed
four-wheeled car is
exemplified by No.116,
seen on dustbin day at
Queens Cross depot.
Several of this type
lasted until the end of
the tramways, their
high ground clearance
making them more
satisfactory for
operation through
snow than were the
bogie cars.

[W. J. Wyse]

DUNDEE This hilly city lost its trams in 1955/6. The system was operated by a fleet of 56 four-wheeled double-deckers, whose well-kept livery of green and cream, lined out in gold, with red glass toplights and maroon trucks, was considered to be among the smartest in the country in the post-war years. The advertisements were a latter-day disfigurement. Car No.28 of 1930 was the newest tram in the fleet, and is depicted at Lochee in virtually original condition apart from the Fischer bow collector which replaced trolley poles in Dundee from 1934.

54

No.44 is standing at Maryfield terminus, not far from the main depot, at the top of one of the hills for which the system was noteworthy. This car was built in 1920 without driver's screens and with open verandah ends to the top deck, but was converted to totally enclosed in the early 1930s.

Tram No.7 started life in Dundee as a bogie open-topper in 1900. It later received a short top cover, and was rebuilt in 1930, becoming a totally enclosed four-wheel car in the process. It is seen at Blackness terminus, and like No.28 opposite has an E.M.B. flexible-axle truck of 8ft. 6in. wheelbase.

SWANSEA & MUMBLES The Mumbles Railway connected Swansea with Mumbles Pier, and ran for most of its length along the shores of Swansea Bay. It was electrified in 1928/9 but its predecessor company carried passengers in 1807 and it is generally acknowledged to have been the first passenger railway in the world. Horse traction was used until replaced by steam in 1877, and various unlikely forms of propulsion such as sails were also experimented with! The electric trams dating from 1928 were the largest in Britain, carrying 106 passengers and normally working in pairs. Livery was red and cream with silver roof, and they only had doors on the landward side. The line closed in 1960 and regrettably none of the cars have survived.

LLANDUDNO The Llandudno & Colwyn Bay Electric Railway connected the two towns by means of a 3ft. 6in. gauge electric tramway, on street track at each end but on private right of way or reserved track on the out-of-town section which took the ascent of the Little Orme in its stride. It opened in 1907 and closed in 1956. The system was latterly worked mainly by secondhand cars, No.2 being one of the Brush maximum-traction bogie single-deckers obtained from Accrington in 1931. Livery was green and cream.

No.11, seen in the main street of Colwyn Bay, was one of ten open-top double-deckers purchased from Bournemouth in 1936; they had Brill 22E bogies and most had bodies by Brush, being built between 1914 and 1926. Happily one has been preserved, and after exhibition in the late lamented Museum of British Transport at Clapham, has now returned to Bournemouth for restoration to its original livery.

Llandudno & Colwyn Bay had four of these 60-seater open 'toastracks', built by English Electric about 1920 on Mountain & Gibson type bogies. They were very similar to the larger standard-gauge cars supplied to Blackpool which were withdrawn in the early 1940s. The Llandudno cars however lasted until the line closed in 1956, and No.21 was photographed at Rhos-on-Sea during a private tour, on a stretch of line so close to the sea that one track had to be closed due to erosion. [W. J. Wyse]

Two impressive streamlined bogie centre-entrance cars were built in 1936/7 for Darwen Corporation, and sold in 1946 to the Llandudno & Colwyn Bay line, who had them regauged from 4ft. 0in. to 3ft. 6in. They were unfortunately only permitted by the Ministry of Transport to carry passengers on the level stretches at each end of the line, and so apart from occasional short workings spent most of their time in the depot. No.24 was captured on one of its forays to Colwyn Bay.

[W. J. Wyse]   61

BELFAST The tramways of Belfast were of the standard 4ft. 8½in. gauge, rather than the 5ft. 3in. favoured by the railways in Ireland. Conversion to trolleybuses commenced in 1938, but the last trams did not run until 1954. The most modern cars in the fleet were the McCreary type, such as No.429, built in the mid-1930s and painted in the attractive blue and cream livery adopted by Belfast in 1929.   [W. J. Wyse]

Belfast as well as Leeds had cars designed by Chamberlain, the Belfast ones being particularly hand-some examples of the traditional British tramcar, as can be seen from this photograph of No.362. They were built in 1930 by Brush on Maley & Taunton swing-link trucks, and several ran until the final closure of the tramways, proving to be more robust than the newer cars. One which escaped the ravages of souvenir hunters on the last day has been preserved in Belfast.   [W. J. Wyse]

Although regular services in Belfast ceased in 1953, peak-hour trams continued to run to Queens Road, serving the shipyards, until February 1954. No.156, an ancient balcony car with the unusual top deck found on the older Belfast cars, was photographed on this route in about 1950. Belfast changed their tram livery from red and cream to blue and cream in 1929, but some of the older cars never received the new colours.

[W. J. Wyse]

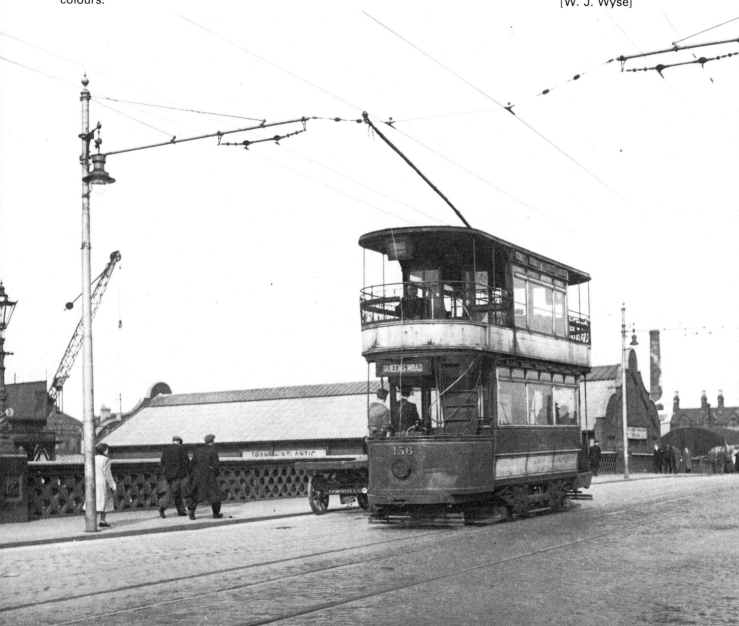

FINTONA The 5ft. 3in. gauge Fintona branch of the Great Northern Railway of Ireland was worked by a horse tram, built in 1883. It originally carried 1st, 2nd and 3rd class passengers, the lower saloon being divided into two halves, and worked until 1957 when the railway closed. The tram is now preserved at Belfast.   [T. B. Owen]

HILL OF HOWTH   This tramway, also of 5ft. 3in. gauge, was situated near Dublin and ran from Sutton to Howth via the Hill of Howth, entirely on reserved track. For most of its life it was operated by the Great Northern Railway of Ireland, and most of its cars carried that company's blue and cream railcar livery. All of its ten cars were open topped, No.2 being built by Brush in 1901 on Brill 22E maximum-traction bogies. The line closed in 1959, and one of the original cars is preserved at Belfast.

66

The final additions to the Hill of Howth tram fleet were Nos.9 and 10, built in 1902 by Milnes on Peckham maximum-traction trucks. These two retained the teak livery with red trucks until withdrawn, and No.10 has been preserved by the Tramway Museum Society. Due to its odd gauge it cannot operate at Crich and is at present in reserve.

THE SURVIVORS

DOUGLAS The famous horse trams still trot along the promenade at Douglas, on the Isle of Man, and celebrated their centenary in 1976. None of the original cars remain, No.36 being one of a batch built in 1896 by Milnes and lengthened in 1908 when it received its end bulkheads.

The 'winter saloons' built by Milnes in 1892 are perhaps the most attractive of the Douglas horse trams. The service has run only in summer since 1927, but the saloons are still used in inclement weather. Like all the surviving cars, they were fitted with roller bearings in 1935/6. No.29 was photographed in Strathallan Crescent, approaching the end of its run.

Horse tram No.46 is a 'bulkhead toastrack' built in 1909 by Milnes, Voss & Co Ltd, while No.18, being manhandled into the depot, was nominally rebuilt from a double-decker. No double-deckers remain in service, but one is preserved in running order, and another very creditable Manx preservation project has been the restoration of one of the cable trams which served Douglas until 1929.

Three 'convertible' cars were supplied by Vulcan in 1935. They are roofed 'toastracks' but can be fitted with side screens in bad weather and the end seat of each bench folded away, thus converting them to saloons. Recent practice has been to keep them in saloon form.

MANX ELECTRIC RAILWAY

The Manx Electric Railway was opened in stages between 1893 and 1899, running from Douglas to Ramsey, though the Laxey–Ramsey section did not operate in 1976 pending a decision as to its future. One of the original 1893 cars, No.2, seen at Douglas in 1961 with 'toastrack' trailer. This remarkable veteran is still serviceable and is in practically original condition apart from having been re-trucked and re-equipped 1903! Livery is red, white, and teak, though a few cars were green and white for a time in the early 1960s.

The newest car in the Manx Electric fleet is No.33, built in 1906 together with matching trailer No.61 by the United Electric Car Co Ltd of Preston. The bench seats extend right across the car, and the conductor has to work from the footboards. This view was taken on a picturesque stretch of line at Fairy Cottage, of cars heading out of Laxey bound for Douglas.

'Winter Saloon' No.20 is one of four built in 1899 by G. F. Milnes & Co Ltd for the through service to Ramsey. The corner entrance is a Manx peculiarity which was also at one time to be found on cars of the Blackpool and Fleetwood Tramroad. The trailer is 'toastrack' No.41, built in 1930 to replace some of the stock lost when Laxey depot burned down.

Seen rounding the horseshoe bend into Laxey from the Ramsey direction are 1894 car No.9 and special saloon No.59, one year newer. No.9 is another product of G. F. Milnes & Co Ltd and received new bogies and equipment in 1903. The trailer was originally a four-wheeler, but was fitted with a pair of spare bogies in 1900.

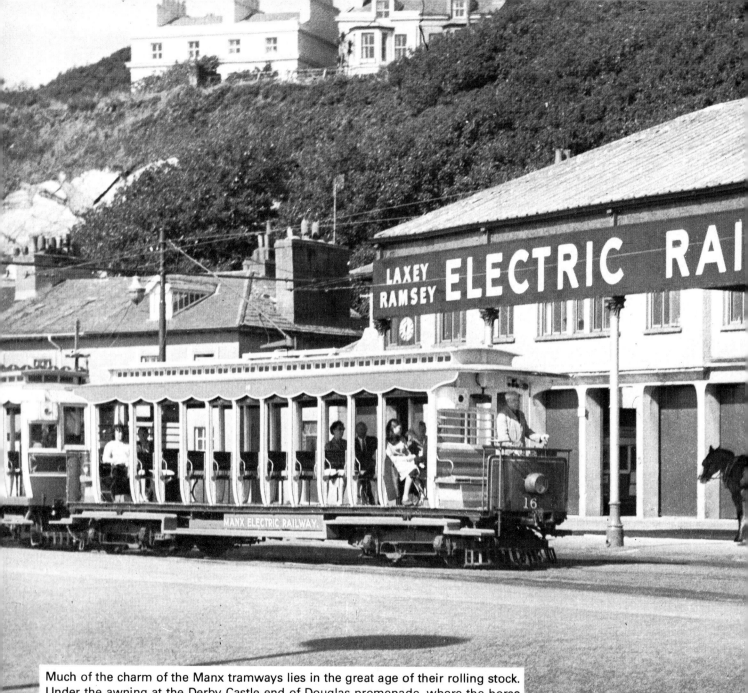

Much of the charm of the Manx tramways lies in the great age of their rolling stock. Under the awning at the Derby Castle end of Douglas promenade, where the horse trams meet those of the Manx Electric at their respective termini, are Manx Electric No. 16 of 1898 and horse tram No. 43 of 1907. This view was taken in 1961, as were most of the Manx illustrations.

SNAEFELL The 3ft. 6in. gauge Snaefell Mountain Railway was opened in 1895, and runs from Laxey, where it connects with the Manx Electric Railway, to the summit of Snaefell, which is the highest point on the Isle of Man. The original six cars, built by Milnes, are still at work but are to be rebuilt with modern electrical equipment, taken from Aachen tramcars, by London Transport Engineering Services! The centre Fell rail, used for braking purposes only, is visible in the picture of No.5 approaching Laxey.

GREAT ORME A cable tramway, opened in 1902, runs from Llandudno to the summit of the Great Orme (679'). The line is worked in two sections, with two cars on each, with a winding house half way. The lower section is very steep and is laid mainly in the streets, with the cable underground. The upper stretch runs across country, with the cable exposed. The cars, which were built by Hurst, Nelson & Co in 1902/3, are in blue and white livery, and have unglazed windows. The overhead wires and trolley poles are only for communication purposes. Car No.4 was photographed on a wet day at the steepest point of the line, and No.7 stands at the halfway station having just arrived from the mist-shrouded summit.

BLACKPOOL Electric trams have run in Blackpool since 1885, the conduit system of collection being used until 1899. Now, Blackpool has Britain's only remaining standard gauge tramway – apart from the museums – and although several routes have closed and the size of the fleet has been much reduced, trams continue to run from Starr Gate, along the whole length of Blackpool's promenade, and then across country to Fleetwood. This picture, taken from the top of a double-decker on a busy summer day, shows in the foreground one of the open 'boat' single-deckers built by English Electric in 1934/5 for Promenade and Circular tours. Originally twelve in number, some have now been withdrawn, and two have gone to the United States on loan.   [B. R. Turner]

These 'standard' bogie double-deckers were built between 1923 and 1929, mostly by Blackpool C.T., but some by Hurst, Nelson & Co. The driver was originally exposed to the elements, but vestibule screens were soon fitted. Not all however received fully enclosed top decks, some retaining their attractive open balconies as seen on No.40, photographed at Pleasure Beach alongside No.160 which had become dewired. The last three cars survived until 1966, and examples of both varieties have been preserved. Livery was originally red and white, but became green and cream in 1933/4.

[B. R. Turner]

The service between Blackpool North Station and Fleetwood was for many years provided by ten bogie single-deckers built in 1928/9 by English Electric. Most were retrucked in 1950/1 and remained in service until 1961. One is preserved, though not yet restored, and others were used as the bases for illuminated feature cars. No.171 was photographed at Cleveleys in 1960.

No.2 is a 'toastrack' car of the former Blackpool & Fleetwood Tramroad Co Ltd, which the Corporation
took over in 1920. It was built in 1898, and after 40 years of service and 20 years of use as a works car, was
restored in 1960 in connection with the tramways 75th anniversary. It was photographed near Gynn
Square about that time, but since 1963 has been at Crich Tramway Museum where it has seen regular
use. [B. R. Turner]

In 1933/4, a series of 25 new single-deckers of revolutionary design were built by English Electric, having centre
doors, two saloons each of 24 seats, separate drivers' cabs, heaters, sunshine roofs, and even clocks in the saloons.
These cars came to be known as 'railcoaches', and future deliveries were of the same general layout. Most gave 30
years service and were scrapped in 1963-5, but No.224, the subject of these reflections, lasted until 1971 – and even
then parts of it were used in the construction of a new car. [B. R. Turner]

Still very much with us are the 27 streamlined double-deckers built by English Electric in 1934/5. They too have centre entrances, with separate drivers' cabs and twin staircases. Sunshine roofs were provided on some, but on others the top decks as built were open, not being enclosed until 1941/2. Some cars have been modified with a single destination box, and seating varies between 84 and 94. There is no railway at Bispham Station, where this night view of No.714 was taken – it is a tram station. [B. R. Turner]

Twenty 'railcoaches' were built by Brush in 1937 on E.M.B. bogies, and most are still in service, but have been modified over the years. As built, they had sliding roofs but these have been replaced by normal roofs on most. Their original air-operated sliding doors used to shut rather powerfully, and these have now been converted to hand operation. Some cars have had single destination boxes fitted, while the controllers and heating systems currently fitted are not the originals. No.297, photographed on the Lytham Road route shortly before it closed in 1961, retains most of its original features.
[B. R. Turner]

Twenty five 'Coronation' bogie single-deckers were built in 1952/3 by Charles Roberts of Horbury on Maley & Taunton inside-bearing bogies, and although extremely handsome cars, they were very heavy and had non-standard electrical equipment which made them expensive to maintain. No.320 was photographed at Fleetwood Ferry in Coronation year, and it is ironic that the last of these cars was withdrawn in Jubilee year.

In 1960/1, ten of Blackpool's 1935-vintage English Electric railcoaches were rebuilt for trailer haulage, and ten trailer were built by Metro-Cammell Weymann, of which five were later fitted with driving controls. They were known as th 'Progress Twin Cars', a name which some of them actually carried, and our photograph shows a pair in Fleetwood o a limited-stop service to Pleasure Beach in the early 1960s. [B. R. Turner]

Two of the modified 1937 railcoaches seen at Starr Gate terminus. No.638 (formerly 302) was rebuilt in 1969 as a 'one-man' car with additional front door, while No.622 (formerly 285) carries unsightly roof-mounted illuminated advertisement displays—which at least provide a source of much-needed additional revenue. [B. R. Turner]

Centre-entrance trams do not readily lend themselves to one-man operation, and over the last few years thirteen of the 1934/5 railcoaches have been dismantled and parts used in the construction of new one-man cars with large front entrances and painted in a distinctive new livery of yellow and red. Pantographs have been experimentally fitted to some.

[B. R. Turner]

Blackpool have for the last 50 years featured illuminated trams, the current fleet including the Blackpool Belle, Tramnik One, Santa Fé Train, Hovertram, and H.M.S. Blackpool. This photograph is of the Blackpool Belle on a daytime cruise at Talbot Square.

[B. R. Turner]

For many years, the television companies filmed the Blackpool Illuminations from two specially-adapted trams. The 'Television Twins' started life in 1927 as open toastracks for the Circular and Promenade Tours, but fell into disuse after the outbreak of war until gaining a new lease of life as mobile camera stands. They are not now used as such, and one has been fully restored to original condition at Crich Tramway Museum.

[B. R. Turner]

TRAMWAYS FOR LEISURE AND PLEASURE

SEATON A 2ft. 9in. gauge tramway runs from Seaton to Colyton, mainly on the course of the former BR branch line, but with an extension into the main car park at Seaton. It is operated by Modern Electric Tramways Ltd, who transferred their stock and equipment from the 2ft. gauge line at Eastbourne which closed in 1969. There are four double-deck and two single-deck cars, about two-thirds full size, in the fleet at present. The upper view shows single-decker No.12 in a passing loop, with the depot beyond.

[C. H. S. Owen]

Power on the Seaton tramway was at first taken from batteries on a flat truc towed by the trams, but nov poles and overhead are erected most of the way to Colyton, and current is taken in the normal manner. At Colyford, where the photograph on the opposite page was taken, the line crosses the A3052 main road on an ungated crossing, though at the time of writing cars had not yet commenced working regularly past this point. [C. H. S. Owen

The Seaton permanent way train, with works car No.02 at the head. The line runs alongside the estuary of the River Axe for most of its length, and is a mecca for bird watchers as well as tram enthusiasts.

COTSWOLD MARINA   A little-known tramway serves the Cotswold Marina, a boating and leisure complex near South Cerney, between Cirencester and Swindon. It is only about a mile long, and of metre gauge, employing diesel traction in the form of a small locomotive previously used in the dockyard at Gibraltar. This tows three tramcar trailers obtained secondhand in 1973 from Charleroi in Belgium.   [T. B. Owen]

EASTBOURNE   The Eastbourne tramway was a 2ft. gauge line of post-war construction, which ran from Princes Park to the Crumbles. Its course was eventually required for road widening, and it closed in 1969. Car No.2 was constructed in 1964, and still runs at Seaton. The unusual staircase arrangement is reminiscent of the design adopted by the former London United Tramways company.   [T. B. Owen]

TRAMWAY PRESERVATION

CARLTON COLVILLE The East Anglian Transport Museum situated at Carlton Colville near Lowestoft has operated a public tram service since 1972 and is the home of Lowestoft tram No.14 plus cars from London, Blackpool and Glasgow. The Lowestoft car was built in 1904 by G. F. Milnes & Co, and ran until the tramways closed in 1931. After many years of static use, it was rescued and is being rebuilt and restored at the Museum, which has recently been extending its depot.   [C. H. S. Owen]

BEAMISH The North of England Open-Air Museum at Beamish in County Durham incorporates a working tramway which was opened in 1973. Bogie car No.10 is a former Gateshead & District Tramways Company vehicle, built in 1925 by their own workshops on Brill 39E maximum-traction bogies. When the Gateshead tramways closed in 1951, No.10 was one of nineteen cars sold to British Railways and ran between Grimsby and Immingham until 1961, receiving malachite green livery and 'lion and wheel' emblem. This car was restored to its crimson and white Gateshead livery after several years in store under the wing of the Museum of British Transport.
[C. H. S. Owen]

CRICH The Tramway Museum at Crich in Derbyshire houses a magnificent collection of about 40 trams, mostly fully restored and in working order, plus a number of others in reserve storage. They operate on ¾ mile of track, and there are long-term possibilities of further extension. Blackpool 'Dreadnought' No.59, built in 1901, is a most unusual car, having twin staircases at each end with a retractable step running the whole width of the car. After 25 years in store, it was restored in 1960 for Blackpool's '75 years of Tramways' celebrations, and later loaned to Crich. It has now returned to Blackpool.

Southampton No.45 was built in 1903 by Hurst Nelson & Co with a low-profile body having one longitudinal back-to-back seat on the top deck. It was so designed to pass through the Bargate at Southampton, and when the tramway there was closed at the end of 1949 it became the first car to be preserved by the Tramway Museum Society. It was one of the first cars to operate at Crich, but has not seen much service in recent years.

Blackpool No.166 is an open 'toastrack' built in 1927 to the same general design as cars dating from 1911-4. Until 1939 at least, the thirty cars of this type operated on the popular Promenade and Circular tours, but most were scrapped during the war years and the few remaining were stored for many years until they too were scrapped or converted to works cars. 166 became a mobile television camera stand in 1953, and in 1972 was donated to the Tramway Museum Society at Crich, reconverted to original condition, and put into service in 1974.

ohannesburg No.60 is one of the four cars at Crich which have come from abroad. It was built in England
n 1906 by the United Electric Car Co Ltd of Preston, originally having a three-window lower saloon. The
ohannesburg tramways ceased operation in 1961, and No.60 was shipped to England in 1964. It has
ppeared in various film and television productions and for several years was the only tram at Crich with
he open-balcony top deck, once so typical of British tramway practice.

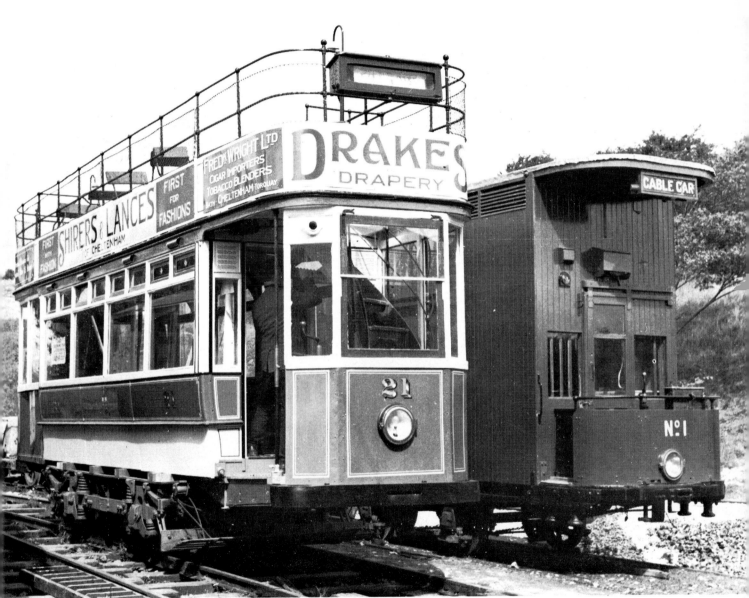

Cheltenham No.21 is representative of the four-wheeled, open-topped cars which worked on the 3ft. 6in. gauge
tramways in the West of England. It was built by English Electric in 1921, and after the Cheltenham & District Light
Railways closed at the end of 1930 its body was used on a farm until rescued and restored by enthusiasts in the early
1960s. It is seen at Crich temporarily mounted on an unmotored standard gauge truck. 'Cable Car No. 1' was not in
fact a cable-operated vehicle, but laid electrical cables for Glasgow's Mains Department.

TYNE & WEAR METRO   Though not a tramway in the accepted sense of the word, the Tyne & Wear Metro which is at present under construction deserves more than passing mention, as its characteristics will be very similar to those of the 'Stadtbahn' systems in Germany which have been developed directly from the town tramway systems. These have been gradually upgraded, placed on reservations and in subways, and re-equipped with new, lightweight, one-man operated rolling stock. The Tyne & Wear Metro is being built largely on former railway right-of-way, but there are also considerable new works including bridges and tunnels. Two prototype trains are already running on a test track.

[Tyne & Wear P.T.E.]   95